WARHAMMER
AGE OF SIGMAR

From the maelstrom of a sundered world, the Eight Realms were born. The formless and the divine exploded into life. Strange, new worlds appeared in the firmament, each one gilded with spirits, gods and men. Noblest of the gods was Sigmar. For years beyond reckoning he illuminated the realms, wreathed in light and majesty as he carved out his reign. His strength was the power of thunder. His wisdom was infinite. Mortal and immortal alike kneeled before his lofty throne. Great empires rose and, for a while, treachery was banished. Sigmar claimed the land and sky as his own and ruled over a glorious age of myth.

But cruelty is tenacious. As had been foreseen, the great alliance of gods and men tore itself apart. Myth and legend crumbled into Chaos. Darkness flooded the realms. Torture, slavery and fear replaced the glory that came before. Sigmar turned his back on the mortal kingdoms, disgusted by their fate. He fixed his gaze instead on the remains of the world he had lost long ago, brooding over its charred core, searching endlessly for a sign of hope. And then, in the dark heat of his rage, he caught a glimpse of something magnificent. He pictured a weapon born of the heavens. A beacon powerful enough to pierce the endless night. An army hewn from everything he had lost. Sigmar set his artisans to work and for long ages they toiled, striving to harness the power of the stars. As Sigmar's great work neared completion, he turned back to the realms and saw that the dominion of Chaos was almost complete. The hour for vengeance had come. Finally, with lightning blazing across his brow, he stepped forth to unleash his creation.

The Age of Sigmar had begun.

HOW TO USE THIS BOOK

Mighty armies clash on a daily basis in the Mortal Realms, but sometimes the outcome of a war is determined by the actions of a few daring individuals. This is *Warhammer Age of Sigmar: Skirmish* – tense, small-scale battles between warbands of brave warriors vying for unimaginable power.

The Mortal Realms are rife with war and death on a truly terrifying scale. Traversing the arcane Realmgates that span the void between worlds, vast campaigning armies endlessly march to war in a conflict as old as the world-that-was. Yet not all battles are fought as large, sweeping engagements; vicious street-fights can erupt over looting rights as opposing warbands pick over the wreckage of lost civilisations, and blood can be spilled as rival chieftains seek to prove their superiority or protect their territory.

Skirmish games put you in command of one such warband of warriors, whose skill, wit and determination are put to the test as they venture into the far-flung reaches of the realms in pursuit of power, riches and glory. Though many of the warriors that comprise a warband would normally form up as a single unit in battle, such a show of strength would prove unwieldy and see them easily outmanoeuvred in small-scale engagements. As such, each general must trust their warriors to fight as individuals as they stalk their way through ruins and tangled forests to lay low rival warbands and search for treasures that will grant their masters a great advantage in the wider conflict.

SKIRMISH RULES

This book contains all the information you'll need to fight Skirmish battles, including rules for selecting your warband and generating unique command abilities and artefacts of power for the hero that leads them. These abilities, such as Merciless Killer or Tenacious Defender, help to

WARBAND ROSTER

This book includes a handy Warband Roster that you can photocopy and use to prepare your warband for the battles ahead. Indeed, your general's quest for glory starts right here!

If you are playing a campaign, then using the Warband Roster will be even more helpful for keeping track of your warband's progress as they fight for power and lost treasures. As your general earns additional command traits or uncovers more ancient artefacts, you can mark down the powerful abilities granted to them. Meanwhile, as your warband grows in size, you can more easily track which new warscrolls your warband's recruits are drawn from.

As your general's legend grows, you will earn renown, which is used to add new warriors to your warband. It is important to know how much renown you have spent and how much you have saved, as this is also a fundamental part of establishing any underdog bonuses in your next game. Thankfully, the Warband Roster has a convenient section to make this process straightforward, as well as a section that serves as a reminder for any triumphs that your warband has earned in preparation for your next game.

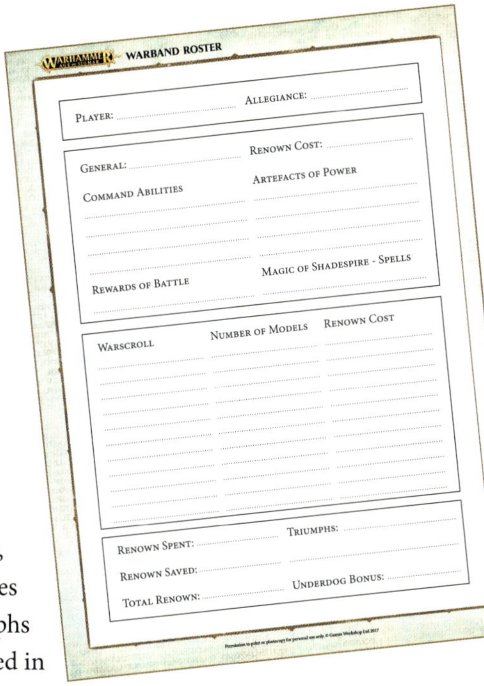
WARBAND ROSTER

Player: Allegiance:

General: Renown Cost:

Command Abilities

Artefacts of Power

Rewards of Battle

Magic of Shadespire - Spells

Warscroll	Number of Models	Renown Cost

Renown Spent: Triumphs:

Renown Saved:

Total Renown: Underdog Bonus:

personalise your warband's general and better represent the backstory you will undoubtedly want to create for them!

SKIRMISH BATTLEPLANS & SHADESPIRE CAMPAIGN

The Skirmish rules have been designed to work with any battleplan, but in this book you will find a set of six new battleplans designed specially for Skirmish battles. These can each be played as one-off games just like any other battleplan, but we have also included rules that allow you to play them in a campaign for two players. The campaign in this book is set within the cursed ruins of Shadespire – the tragic story of which you can read over the next few pages – but there is no reason why you couldn't use the rules as a framework to create a campaign based elsewhere in the realms.

After taking part in a Skirmish campaign, your warband will also be comfortably large enough to take part in a Path to Glory campaign, which is the perfect follow-up to your collecting, painting and gaming journey. For more information on Path to Glory campaigns, see the *General's Handbook*.

MATCHED PLAY

Skirmish battles present very different tactical scenarios to large-scale battles. As such, the Pitched Battle profiles in the *General's Handbook* don't apply to Skirmish games. Instead, Skirmish battles use a system of 'renown' to indicate the relative strengths of different miniatures. The tables at the back of this book list the miniatures you can take in Skirmish warbands, along with their associated renown costs. There's also a section on page 21 that contains helpful advice on matched play for Skirmish battles, providing you with plenty of tools for balancing your games.

MUSTERING YOUR WARBAND

The smaller size of Skirmish battles provides hobbyists with a great opportunity to devote more time to individual miniatures. Many players will want to create backstories for the warriors in their warband and convert them with parts from their bits box to bring out their personalities. Collecting a warband is also a great opportunity to try out new techniques and colour schemes without having to commit to doing a whole army in a given style.

For the tactically minded, the short, sharp nature of Skirmish battles lends itself to all manner of enjoyable game variations. As the action is swift, you can get several battles in during the course of the same session! Get started with the six battleplans found within these pages, but there is no reason your battles have to end there. The vastness of the Mortal Realms offers endless potential, so what are you waiting for?

VENGEANCE OF AZYR

With a crack of thunder the Gates of Azyr opened and the Age of Sigmar was begun. Forged by the God-King, the Stormcast Eternals strode forth to drive back the encroaching hordes of Chaos, and in bloody battle they gave hope of salvation to the beleaguered realms.

In the distant past, Sigmar forged a Great Alliance with his fellow gods, and they imposed their divine will upon the Mortal Realms. Together, they freed the Realmgates from the tyrannical beasts that roamed the lands, allowing humans, aelves and duardin to come together. These mortals built mighty civilisations replete with magic and great wonders, and they flourished in this time of abundance. Yet with each passing generation, Sigmar's pantheon grew ever more frayed, and eventually it was torn apart from within.

Each of the gods abandoned or betrayed Sigmar, turning upon one another or sequestering themselves in their own domains. Gorkamorka, the bellicose god of the greenskins, launched a ferocious Waaagh! that raged from one end of the Eight Realms to the other. Alarielle the Everqueen retreated deep into the glades of Ghyran, where she tended only to her own people. Nagash set his undead legions upon Sigmar's armies at the Allpoints. As the God-King in his righteous fury marched into Shyish to deliver retribution to the Great Necromancer, the malignant influence of the Chaos Gods grew stronger.

The influence of the Ruinous Powers began to seep into the Mortal Realms, slowly at first, then like a tidal wave crushing all in its path. The Age of Chaos erupted violently into being as daemons and savage barbarians laid waste to the civilised world. Entire nations were butchered, their fields sown with rancid gore so that no living thing would grow in them again.

Enormous walled cities were ground to dust beneath the cloven hoofs of malformed monstrosities, and colossal statues enshrining the triumphs of mortal heroes were torn down, melted and reforged as graven images of the Dark Gods. Libraries, map rooms and schools of the arcane were desecrated, and knowledge that had been gathered over centuries was lost forever.

In those bleak days Sigmar retreated to Azyrheim, and from there he set about forging his greatest weapon – the Stormcast Eternals. The most resolute mortal heroes were spirited from across the realms to the God-King's side, where they were imbued with a portion of his righteous fury. They would be the last bulwark against the inexorable tide of the Ruinous Powers.

It was in Aqshy that the Stormhosts were first unleashed against Khorne's mortal legions. The Hammers of Sigmar, cast down from the Heavens upon bolts of lightning, brought vengeance to the Blood God's savage minions and opened the long-sealed Gates of Azyr. In Ghyran and Chamon, the Stormcast Eternals marched to battle against Nurgle and Tzeentch, and in the lands they reclaimed were found allies thought to have been lost.

With Sigmar's alliance reforming, the Stormcast Eternals set out to capture the sundered Realmgates connecting disparate kingdoms. Droves of daemons fell beneath their hammer blows, and the foul blood of idolaters flowed wherever the Stormhosts marched. Mighty though they were, the Stormcasts were not completely invulnerable, and upon death they would return to Azyr in a burst of energy, ready to be reforged and sent once more into battle. Though their bodies were preserved in this way, each Reforging stripped them of some small part of their essence and dimmed the flame of their heroic souls.

The Stormcast Eternals and their allies have stemmed the tide of ruin, but their hold on the Mortal Realms is far from secure. The legions of Chaos continue to enact the wills of the Dark Gods, while the frothing hordes that worship Gorkamorka still ravage all that they come across. In Shyish, Nagash has maintained his hold over the undead, and with each battle more soldiers are added to his already swollen ranks.

THE MORTAL REALMS

Amidst the dark and formless void are eight pockets of creation. Ageless, immense and saturated with magical energy, they are filled with continent-spanning civilisations, scattered tribes of savages and the followers of ancient gods. These are the Mortal Realms.

Each of the eight Mortal Realms is a separate plane of reality, vast beyond comprehension and ancient as the stars. It was Dracothion that found Sigmar drifting through the endless void, borne upon the core of a dead world. The Great Drake showed the God-King hidden paths that connected the realms, and Sigmar explored them on great voyages of discovery. He found primitive tribes and other gods such as himself, lost and alone. Sigmar roused the gods and led them to claim dominion over the places they found.

The immortal will of these beings gave new shape to the realms, though each plane has forever remained an incarnation of magic – a separate expression of the fundamental forces of existence. They are the Realms of Fire, Heavens, Metal, Beasts, Light, Shadow, Life and Death.

The innate energy of each plane affects all that resides within them. In Aqshy, the Realm of Fire, the power of flame coalesces into winding spines of volcanic mountains and boiling seas of sulphurous water. The air is thick and heavy, and ash storms come thundering over the horizon blown by super-heated winds. The people of Aqshy are known for their passion and intensity, and their lives burn quick and bright.

Ghyran, the Realm of Life, is filled with growth and abundance. All manner of beings – from humans to sylvaneth to troggoths – live amongst the rampant vegetation. Colossal trees reach into the sky where their leaves drink the clouds. Among their boughs entire cities are

built, replete with gardens and forests of their own, and the denizens of these cities embrace the cycle of life and rebirth that permeates their existence.

The Realm of Death is a desolate and solemn place where all things come to an end. Osseous shrubs and withered trees sprout from barren soil atop mountains of mouldering corpses. Vast savannahs of tesseral tombstones mark the bulging massed graves of the innumerable dead. The living inhabitants of Shyish exist side by side with the unliving, and their cities are warded against the cannibalistic shamblers and restless spirits that linger in the wilds.

Azyr is the Realm of Heavens, and it is here that Sigmar gathered his fellow gods to council. The great city of Azyrheim, illuminated by perpetual starlight, is home to creatures of every race, gathered to serve in the God-King's armies. When the Chaos Gods beset the Mortal Realms, refugees came flooding into Sigmar's city before the Gates of Azyr were shut.

Though separated from one another, each of the realms is connected by Realmgates – ageless portals that bridge the space between worlds. Some are marked by towering stone statues, field-spanning networks of geoglyphs or embellished archways of impossible size. Others are more elusive, and are found within tangled copses of ancient trees or in the darkest recesses of long and twisting caves. In the Age of Chaos, the Ruinous Powers sought to corrupt these portals, diverting their paths so that they led directly to the warped Realm of Chaos. Not only did this stop the armies of mortals from travelling between their lands, but it allowed the daemonic servants of the Dark Gods to pour out into reality.

None were safe from the wars against Chaos, save for those who were sealed in Azyr. Nations were sundered and their people scattered. All seemed lost until the Heavenly Gates were opened once more and the Stormcast Eternals came forth to deliver Sigmar's wrath. But the glimmer of hope is still dim, and could be snuffed out at any moment. The battered and beleaguered people of the Mortal Realms fight for their own survival, and will stop at nothing to secure victory.

SHADESPIRE'S CURSE

Many grand cities arose in the Age of Myth only to be sundered by rampaging armies and the wills of terrifying gods. Few were more glorious than Shadespire – the city amongst the dunes – and fewer still fell so completely and with such rapidity.

Shadespire once stood as a shining metropolis – a beacon of power and prosperity in the grim and withered Realm of Death. Its glass towers glistened with precious stones of every hue, casting iridescent reflections across the surrounding Desert of Bones. Now it is a cold and desiccated husk, stripped of its lustre and utterly cursed. Its once-magnificent spires are little more than crumbling protrusions that claw lifelessly at the bleak sky, while its outer districts are slowly subsumed by the encroaching skeletal dunes that are blown ever inwards. The city has all but faded from memory, and those few who have heard the tales of its former glory speak of it only in fearful whispers. The very name of Shadespire is a curse, and is synonymous with damnation.

In the Age of Myth, the founders of Shadespire set out to create a waypoint in the middle of the Desert of Bones – a safe haven for travellers and merchants on the treacherous journey between distant Realmgates. The enormous desert was anathema to life as the perilous gusts of the Wailing Wind would strip flesh from bone and carry the aetheric essence of a body away to the Silent Wastes, but amidst the shifting mountains of lifeless remains, the Oasis of Souls was found. This twisting network of canyons cut deep into the compacted bone sediment beneath the dunes, descending far further into the darkness than those who discovered it dared venture. They knew not what had formed this plunging abyss, but the wisest amongst them believed it to be a locus through which the flowing energies of Shyish converged. Perhaps the morbid ley lines cancelled each other out at this point, preventing the death-soaked earth from coalescing, or perhaps the conflux of grim magic caused the realm itself to waste away here under the unbearable weight

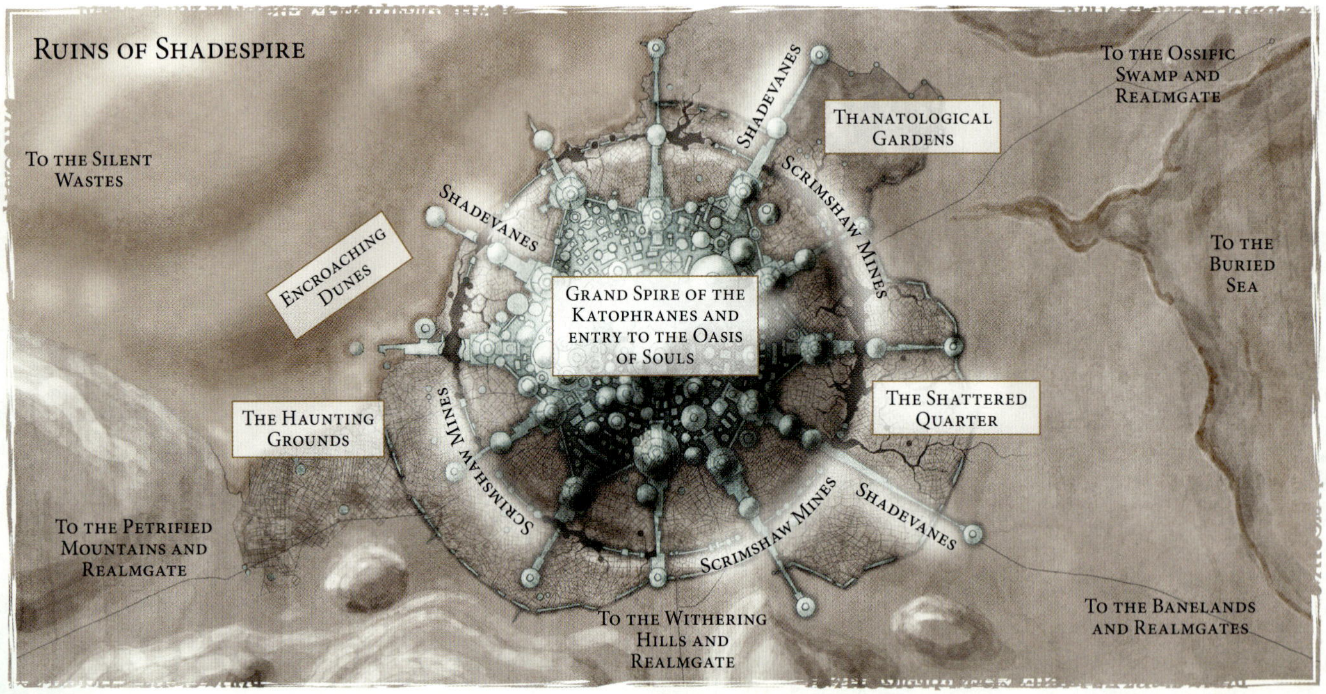

of moribund energy. Whatever its nature, shelter was found within the many recesses of the Oasis, as was water and stubborn patches of Shyish's anaemic vegetation. As the first weary vagabonds explored the caves further, they found their spirits invigorated – bolstered against the surrounding lifelessness when in the presence of the inky-black ores that ran in seams through the caverns. It was from this place of respite that the first shanties and stores of Shadespire arose.

The waypoint quickly became a town, which then became a bustling hub of commerce and culture, with humans, aelves and duardin from every corner of the realms passing through its gates. Massive towers were built at the centre of the burgeoning city, which could be seen far off into the surrounding barrens. The wonders of distant lands were brought to Shadespire to be traded, and sharp-eyed collectors scoured its market squares for esoteric tomes of knowledge and curiosities imbued with magic. The weaponry and spellcraft of a thousand kingdoms was brought inside the city walls, and here it was combined, adapted and refined to produce artefacts of unequalled power. The ingenious creators who were able to craft such objects were rewarded with riches and vaunted in Shadespire's high courts. A ruling elite emerged known as the Katophranes, and their glory continued to expand with their boundless innovation. All paid tithes to the Katophranes for the privilege of entering their city, and emperors and warlords alike bowed in deference to their might, entreating them for tools to help them conquer new lands.

The Katophranes' greatest work was the crafting of glass made from the dark ores within the Oasis of Souls. Shadeglass, as they called it, could capture the essence of one's being at the point of death, before the soul seeped away to the Underworlds. With shadeglass, the knowledge and memories of the dying could be preserved, and the Katophranes were able to live beyond their mortal years as pure thought, unshackled from their aging bodies. Exquisitely crafted mirrors and illuminated panes were given places of prominence throughout the city, all of which were connected by the crystalline monument known as the Faneway, the nexus through which all soul energy passed. The Katophranes, preserved within their prisms, communed with one another and oversaw their city, and together they revelled in the powers they had mastered. In the middle of a lifeless wasteland, in the Amethyst Realm itself, they had conquered death, and in doing so they roused the undying wrath of Nagash.

NAGASH, GOD OF THE DEAD

From the cold stillness of the Underworlds, the Great Necromancer cast his spiteful gaze upon Shadespire. For too long had the Katophranes received tributes from others while at the same time denying Nagash his rightful tithe of souls. This was an insult that could not be borne, and the god weaved a hateful spell, drawing upon the power of the shadeglass that was sown throughout the city. The inhabitants of Shadespire would not simply be executed for their heinous debt – for those who had tried to deny death there would be a far greater punishment. As Nagash unleashed his sorcery, the soul of Shadespire was severed from reality. Every living creature within the city was siphoned into oblivion, leaving no trace of their existence save for the desolate ruin they once called home.

TREASURES OF THE KATOPHRANES

The remnants of Shadespire lie forgotten in the Desert of Bones. Each year, more of the city succumbs to the harrows of age, and more of its buildings disappear beneath the towering dunes. Its former glory has been utterly excised, yet the wealth that it held is still there for the taking.

When the soul of Shadespire was stolen by Nagash, those kingdoms that had traded with the desert city cowered in fear, wondering if the Great Necromancer's wrath would also fall upon their territories. Returning envoys who had left Shadespire before its demise were slaughtered upon reaching their homelands, a precaution lest they carried with them a portion of the god's curse. Tomes of lore concerning the city were put to the torch, and to utter its name was deemed a blasphemy – an affront to Nagash that was punishable by a torturous death. Shadespire and the Katophranes were spoken of no more, and in time both ebbed into legend.

Though forgotten, and reduced to a hollow skeleton of the metropolis it once was, Shadespire still lies where it died in the desert. The abundant treasures that had been collected by the city's living inhabitants for countless generations remain untouched. Within its mausolean halls lies the wealth of untold empires, paid to the Katophranes to procure but a modicum of their profound wisdom. Gemstones gouged from mines in Aqshy and gold ingots from the hills of Chamon sit nestled amongst piles of gathering bone-dust. The works of master artisans are scattered haphazardly through buildings that have thus far withstood the erosion of malevolent gales. Even in the poorer suburbs and the outright slums, small ensorcelled trinkets sit on tables in the gaunt abodes that have not yet been buried under the roving mountains of desiccated remains. So plentiful were these riches during Shadespire's ascendency that they distracted the roaming eyes of the city's many supplicants from the true treasures that lay secreted beneath the surface.

The greatest creations of the Katophranes still reside in hidden chambers carved into the osseous bedrock, sealed behind ornate cog-work doors that bar entry to those who do not know their secrets. Libraries of

REFLECTIONS OF DEATH

Across the centuries, among people scattered throughout the Mortal Realms, rumours of the Katophranes' fate have persisted. Most of these exist as folk legends about a great, mirrored city, and serve as a warning to the listener about the dangers of displeasing the Lord of the Dead. With time, the names and details have become clouded, but all tell of the Katophranes' extravagant wealth, their incomparable ingenuity and their ultimate hubris.

A rare few claim to have crossed the deadly dunes, to have found the desolated city and to have returned alive. They talk of a haunted place where the people of Shadespire once lived, still heavy with the fell power of Nagash. They tell of their companions vanishing without trace in the winding alleys of the dread city, leaving no body or worldly possessions to be found. Most chilling are stories of the shattered shadeglass panes littering the streets. In them are glimpsed twisted faces screaming out from a dim illusion of the city that once was. They appear briefly before disappearing, leaving only a foreboding reflection of the beholder.

the arcane lie behind lock and key, their shelves packed with tomes of lore harvested from the greatest scholars of the realms. Unnavigable labyrinths lead to vast alchemical laboratories that, despite the passage of time, still hum with the slowly bleeding power of transmuted metals. In the sprawling outer districts, below watch-houses that dot the barren streets, weapons engraved with complex runes line the racks of secure armouries, their innate magic shielding them from the gnawing effects of corrosion.

No treasure was more precious than the knowledge of shadeglass. The encrypted tomes that record the process of its crafting and the implements with which it was fashioned are still guarded by the deadliest designs of the Katophranes. The fractal passages that were built to

access the shadeglass foundries deep within the Oasis of Souls confound those without knowledge of their construction. Elaborate blade-traps set in the joins of seemingly mundane masonry still wait to be sprung, having lost none of their lethal potency over the passing centuries. Sorcerous wards and golems laced with veins of ur-gold wait in silence to be activated by those who do not have the permission of their creators to pass. The Katophranes went to great lengths to protect their most sacred discovery, and though they kept its secrets, the damnation they incurred was shared with all of Shadespire.

THE HAUNTING GROUNDS

Savage warlords and beleaguered generals alike have begun listening to fragmented rumours about the soulless city that have trickled down through the ages. In these desperate times, few can ignore the stories of the fabled artefacts of power crafted by the Nagash-cursed Katophranes.

As Sigmar and his allies push back against the legions of Chaos, the forces of Destruction and Death continue to bring ruin to the last stubborn remnants of civilisation. On all sides, the power-hungry and the desperate seek new tools of war to shift the teetering balance of power. The ambitions of the embattled are ignited by whispers of Shadespire, of the once-mighty Katophranes and of the treasures that lie waiting in the desert. Stories are told of relics that could win wars across the Mortal Realms – and so, after centuries of silent crumbling, Shadespire has once more become host to the living.

Only the determined survive the long trek through the barren dunes. Scouts and warriors set out in small parties, for the attrition the Desert of Bones would wreak upon an entire army would be too devastating for any general to bear. There are no charts to guide the journeys across the vast wastes. What maps did exist were destroyed long ago, either burned for fear that they carried the taint of Nagash's curse, or torn to shreds by the barbaric followers of the Ruinous Powers.

After months amidst the skeletonising vortexes of the Wailing Wind, the hardy, the guileful and the lucky approach Shadespire. Inside the ancient walls there is even greater peril. Decrepit streets give way to yawning chasms under heavy footfalls, and sepulchral buildings collapse on passers-by without warning as their brittle bone-mortar finally succumbs

to the erosion of time. Those who are separated from their party are cut down in the deadly lattice of traps laid by the Katophranes, or are devoured by the unseen dark forces that still haunt every corner of the city.

By far the greatest threats to a warband are others who have come to Shadespire seeking the same arcane rewards. Every echoing alley is a perfect site for ambush, and every desolate market square a potential battlefield. Roving mobs of mortals, beasts and daemons prowl the wrecked city like scavengers picking clean a colossal corpse. Each is prepared to fight to the last, and should they secure the power they seek, then their enemies will tremble before them, both in Shadespire and in the wars of the Mortal Realms.

Putrid blood dripped from the grandblade of Liberator-Prime Severin Steelheart as the remaining vermin-folk scurried off into the rubble-strewn alleys. Turning, he saw that all of his fellow Stormcast Eternals were still standing. Only six of their chamber had come to Shadespire, but they were dauntless warriors all.

With a silent nod from their leader, Knight-Questor Kantar Gloryborn, Severin and the others fell into step. There was little time to dwell on victories, and there would be many more battles as they searched the sprawling crypt of a city. But as Severin passed the foetid torso of the skaven priest he had just bisected, he spied a glistening shard of dark glass clutched in the ratman's lifeless claw. He stooped low to closer examine the jewel-like object. Its blackness was impenetrable – as deep and as cold as a lifeless ocean. Reaching down he let his armoured finger rest upon its surface, and felt a curious resonance deep within his being. Faces flittered across the facets. Some of these he thought he recognised from a life long ago; others were strange and contorted, as though crying out in agony. This was shadeglass, and the power it held was the reason they had been sent to the cursed city.

SKIRMISH RULES

SKIRMISH BATTLES

SKIRMISH BATTLEPLANS

On pages 22-27 you will find six battleplans designed specifically for Skirmish battles, but with a little modification you can easily use the Skirmish rules with any battleplan. For example, you could use one of the Triumph & Treachery battleplans in the *General's Handbook* to fight a Skirmish battle with more than two players.

THE WARBANDS

To play a Skirmish battle, each player will need to create a warband, which represents the plucky band of adventurers they will be commanding on the battlefield. The full rules for choosing your warband, along with any restrictions that apply when doing so, can be found on page 34.

SKIRMISH FORMATION

In Skirmish battles, all models in your warband fight as individuals rather than cohesive groups. Each model in your warband is therefore treated as single unit, and does not have to obey the usual rules for remaining within 1" of other models from their warscroll. However, the abilities of specific models equipped as a musician or standard bearer (for example, models equipped with a banner, icon, standard or flag, as well as models carrying drums, horns, bells, etc.) still have an effect on friendly models within 6" that are chosen from the same warscroll.

ALLEGIANCE ABILITIES

Every warband owes allegiance to one of the Grand Alliances – either **ORDER**, **CHAOS**, **DEATH** or **DESTRUCTION**. The units you choose to make up your warband may make it eligible for allegiance abilities from a number of different sources, such as battletomes and the *General's Handbook*. However, in a Skirmish battle, your warband can only use the allegiance abilities of the Grand Alliance from which they hail.

THE GENERAL

Each warband is led by a general – a powerful leader that, through cunning or valour, has risen to a prominent position of command. Your general is chosen from the **HEROES** in your warband, as described on page 34.

Your general cannot use the Inspiring Presence command ability found on the *Warhammer Age of Sigmar* rules sheet, though you are free to use any command ability on their warscroll. Alternatively, you can generate a command ability for your general from the table on page 17. In addition, you can equip your general either with an artefact of power from the table on page 17, or one from the artefacts available to their Grand Alliance (see the *General's Handbook).*

BATTLESHOCK TESTS

Do not use the normal rules for the battleshock phase. Instead, in each battleshock phase, a special battleshock test must be taken if any models from your warband have been slain during that turn. The player whose turn it is tests first as normal.

When taking this battleshock test, roll a dice and add the number of models from your warband that were slain that turn. For each point by which the total exceeds your general's Bravery characteristic, one model of your choice from your warband must flee and is removed from play. If your general has been slain, treat your warband as having a Bravery of 5 for this test.

SUMMONED UNITS

Sometimes a spell or ability on a unit's warscroll will allow you to add additional models – sometimes even entire units – to the battlefield, or otherwise replace models that have been destroyed. However, when playing a Skirmish battle, these abilities do not have any effect under any circumstances.

THE THREE RULES OF ONE

The following special rules apply to all Skirmish battle games:

The 1st Rule of One: Each spell can be attempted only once per turn rather than once per wizard per turn. For example, after you have attempted to cast Arcane Bolt, you cannot attempt to cast it again in the same turn.

The 2nd Rule of One: A roll of 1 to hit, wound, or save always fails. This applies to the roll after any re-rolls have been taken, but before modifiers are applied.

The 3rd Rule of One: Any extra attacks, hit rolls or wound rolls gained by the use of an ability cannot themselves generate extra attacks, hit rolls or wound rolls. For example, the extra hit roll generated by a Ripperdactyl's Voracious Appetite ability could not also generate further hit rolls.

COMMAND ABILITIES

Commanding small-scale warbands requires a different style of leadership to directing large armies. Either roll a dice on the following table or pick a command ability that best suits the your general's style of leadership or the backstory you have given them.

COMMAND ABILITIES TABLE

Roll	Command Ability
1	**Inspirational Fighter:** You can re-roll hits rolls of 1 for friendly models within 6" of your general until your next hero phase.
2	**Merciless Killer:** Add 1 to wound rolls you make for friendly models within 6" of your general until your next hero phase.
3	**Reserves of Courage:** You can add 2 to your general's Bravery when taking battleshock tests until your next hero phase.
4	**Crusader:** You can re-roll failed charge rolls for friendly models within 6" of your general until your next hero phase.
5	**Tenacious Defender:** You can re-roll save rolls of 1 for friendly models within 6" of your general until your next hero phase.
6	**Indomitable Will:** You can attempt to unbind one spell in each of your opponent's hero phases until your next hero phase. If your general is a WIZARD, they can attempt to unbind one additional spell in each enemy hero phase instead.

ARTEFACTS OF POWER

Mighty leaders will often bear powerful enchanted weaponry and accoutrements of war. Either roll a dice on the following table or pick an artefact that best suits the appearance of your general or the backstory you have given them.

ARTEFACTS OF POWER TABLE

Roll	Artefact of Power
1	**Blessed Amulet:** Add 1 to your general's Wounds characteristic.
2	**Soulsever Blade:** Pick one of your general's melee weapons – you may re-roll failed wound rolls for that weapon.
3	**Cursed Tome:** Add 1 to any casting rolls you make for your general. However, if your casting roll is a double 1, your general suffers a mortal wound after the spell is resolved.
4	**Oblivion Charm:** If your general is slain, roll a dice for each enemy model within 3" of them before removing the model from the battlefield; on a roll of 4 or more, the model being rolled for suffers a mortal wound.
5	**Masque of Horror:** Your opponent must roll a dice each time they wish to target your general in the combat phase. On a roll of 1, the model being rolled for is paralysed by fear and may not attack this turn.
6	**Helm of Authority:** Once per battle in your hero phase, your general can use one command ability chosen from the table on the left in addition to any others they can use, though you cannot use the same one twice.

MYSTERIOUS TERRAIN

The landscapes of the Mortal Realms vary as much as the multifarious races that dwell there. Once you have set up all your scenery, either roll a dice on the following table to find out what kind of terrain it is, or pick a rule which best suits the scenery piece's appearance.

MYSTERIOUS TERRAIN TABLE

Roll	Scenery
1	**Cursed:** In your hero phase, roll a dice for each of your models within 3" of this terrain feature. On a roll of 1, that model suffers a mortal wound.
2	**Arcane:** Add 1 to the result of any casting or unbinding roll made for a WIZARD within 3" of this terrain feature.
3	**Emboldening:** If your general is within 3" of this terrain feature when you are taking a battleshock test, you can choose to re-roll the result.
4	**Crumbling:** Roll a dice each time one of your models runs or charges within 1" of this terrain feature. On a roll of 1, the terrain feature collapses; the model that triggered the collapse is slain, and the terrain feature is removed from the board.
5	**Enchanted:** In your hero phase, choose one model within 3" of this terrain feature and roll a dice; on a 3 or more you can re-roll failed wound rolls for that model until your next hero phase.
6	**Foreboding:** Players must subtract 1 from any hit rolls they make for models within 3" of this terrain feature.

SHADESPIRE CAMPAIGN RULES

There are many ways to link your games of *Warhammer Age of Sigmar: Skirmish* together. The following rules allow you to play a linear narrative campaign set amidst the ruined city of Shadespire.

This campaign pits two players against one another in a series of six Skirmish battles, the last of which is a winner-takes-all decider to determine the overall victor of the campaign. Playing through a series of games in this manner serves as a fun and exciting way to grow a collection of miniatures whilst developing an ongoing narrative for the leader of your budding army.

Designer's Note: *With a few minor tweaks to the rules presented on these pages, it is simplicity itself to increase the number of players or the duration of the campaign.*

STARTING A CAMPAIGN

To begin a campaign, the players will first need to pick their starting warbands, as described on page 34. We recommend spending no more than 25 renown on each warband at the start of the campaign, as it will increase in size and strength as the campaign unfolds and more warriors are drawn in by your general's fame (or infamy!).

Though the Skirmish battles included on the following pages can all be played individually as one-off games, when played as part of a campaign, each game is played once, in the order shown below.

Game	Battleplan
1	Clash at Dawn (pg 22)
2	Treasure Hunt (pg 23)
3	Fragile Cargo (pg 24)
4	Vortex of Power (pg 25)
5	Assassinate (pg 26)
6	Seize the Relic (pg 27)

Victory in the final game establishes the overall winner of the campaign, so even should one player lose all five of the preceding games, they will still have a chance to snatch victory from the jaws of defeat!

UNDERDOG BONUS

Before each game, players should add up the total renown they have spent on their warband. The player with the lowest total renown is the underdog, and will receive a number of re-rolls in that game according to the difference in renown as follows:

Difference in Renown	Re-rolls
1-10	1
11-20	3
21+	5

These re-rolls can be expended to re-roll any single dice roll you make in any of the following situations:

- Casting roll
- Unbinding roll
- Run roll
- Charge roll
- Hit roll
- Wound roll
- Save roll
- Damage roll
- Battleshock test

BETWEEN GAMES

With the exception of the climactic final battle, the players must resolve these two simple steps after each game to prepare their warband for the next stage of the campaign:

1. Roll on the Rewards of Battle table (pg 19).
2. Earn and spend renown.

EARNING AND SPENDING RENOWN

A general's reputation relies on their ability to win battles, as well as the magnitude of each victory. After each game, players earn additional renown to spend on reinforcing their warband in accordance with the outcome, as shown below:

Result	Renown Earned
Major victory	+10
Minor victory	+8
Draw	+7
Loss	+6

Any renown a warband earns can either be expended immediately to add models to your warband (following all of the rules for choosing your warband on page 34), or retained for future purchases between games. Make a note of any unspent renown on your warband's roster sheet.

CASUALTIES

Any models that were slain or fled during the battle are assumed to either fully recover from their injuries or return to the warband (in shame!) in time for your next game.

Designer's Note: *It is worth pointing out that aside from spending renown to add models to your warband, you cannot change the composition of your warband between games – once a model has joined your warband, they remain part of it for the duration of the campaign.*

REWARDS OF BATTLE

After each game, players can roll on the following table to determine what treasures their warband has uncovered or how much their general's reputation has grown. However, if you won a **major victory** or **minor victory** in your previous game, you can instead roll three dice and pick any two results to make your 2D6 score.

2D6 Reward

2 Fortuitous Trinket: This seemingly mundane object has the power to alter destiny itself. In your next battle, you may re-roll a single dice roll you make for your general.

3 Warding Glyph: Saturated with protective magic, this curious sigil guards against mortal harm. In your next battle, you may roll a dice whenever your general suffers a mortal wound. On a 5+ the wound is ignored.

4 Healing Elixir: Draining this potion can bring the imbiber back from the brink of death. In one of your hero phases in your next battle, your general may heal D3 wounds suffered earlier in that battle.

5 Choose one of the following:
The Trickster's Shard: A spiteful charm of unknown origin. In your next battle, the first time an enemy model successfully unbinds a spell cast by your general, the unbinding model suffers a mortal wound.

The Other Trickster's Shard: Another spiteful charm of unknown origin. In your next battle, the first time an enemy model inflicts an unsaved wound or mortal wound on your general in the combat phase, the attacking model immediately suffers a mortal wound.

6-8 Heroic Saga: Your general's reputation continues to grow. You earn an extra D3 renown.

9 Tactical Insight: Bitter experience in Shadespire has taught your general much. You may randomly generate an additional command ability from the Command Abilities table (pg 17) for your general. If you roll a command ability your general already has, treat this as a Heroic Saga result instead.

10 Ancient Relic: An artefact from the world-that-was grants your general tremendous power. You may randomly generate an additional artefact for your general from the Artefacts of Power table (pg 17), or, if they are a WIZARD, a spell from the Magic of Shadespire table (right). If you roll an artefact or spell that your general already has, treat this as a Heroic Saga result instead.

11 Famed Commander: Fame and fortune are the rewards for those deemed worthy in Shadespire. You earn an extra D6 renown.

12 Legendary Hero: Your general's deeds in Shadespire have become legend. You earn an extra 6 renown.

MAGIC OF SHADESPIRE

If your general is a WIZARD and you roll ' Ancient Relic' result on the Rewards of Battle table (left), you may randomly generate a Shadespire spell for them from this table instead of rolling on the Artefacts of Power table.

D3 Shadespire Spell

1 TWILIGHT PATHWAY
Twilight Pathway has a casting value of 5. If successfully cast, pick a friendly model within 12" of the caster. You may remove that model from the battlefield and place it anywhere that is more than 9" from enemy models. The model may not move in the subsequent movement phase.

2 SHARDMIST
Shardmist has a casting value of 6. If successfully cast, until your next hero phase your opponent must subtract 1 from any hit rolls they make in the shooting phase when targeting the caster or any models within 6" of them.

3 SOUL SIPHON
Soul Siphon has a casting value of 5. If successfully cast, pick a model (friend or foe) within 12" of the caster. That model suffers a mortal wound and the caster immediately heals one wound suffered earlier in the battle. This may not take the caster above their Wounds characteristic.

SHADESPIRE CAMPAIGN

1. SHADESPIRE BECKONS

Your warband has arrived at the outskirts of Shadespire in the dead of night. While looking for a defensible campsite you cross paths with a band of rivals, and as the murky dawn begins to break, battle erupts.

Play Clash at Dawn on page 22.

2. CITY OF THE DEAD

Pushing into the ruins, your warband has come across a series of crypts, each rumoured to contain artefacts of great power. You must stop your rivals from taking these for themselves!

Play Treasure Hunt on page 23. If one of the players was victorious in Clash at Dawn, then they may choose who has the first turn in the first battle round, regardless of who finishes setting up first.

TO THE VICTOR, THE SPOILS!

The winner can randomly generate an artefact of power from the Artefacts of Power table on page 17. If the winner achieved a **major victory**, they can choose an artefact from the table instead.

3. THE ANCIENT WARLORD

Your warband has come across the sarcophagus of a once-great warlord in the middle of a public square. You can try to decipher his secrets from the stone tablets within, but will need to move his cist to safety first!

Play Fragile Cargo on page 24. If one of the players was victorious in Treasure Hunt, then they are automatically the guard and their territory is extended to reach the centre of the battlefield.

TO THE VICTOR, THE SPOILS!

The winner can randomly generate a command ability from the Command Abilities table on page 17. If the winner achieved a **major victory**, they can choose an ability from the table instead.

4. THE SOUL WELL

After intoning the runes on the warlord's tablets, you attempt to channel the energies of a soul well, though your rivals seek to cut you down before the ritual is complete!

Play Vortex of Power on page 25. If one of the players was victorious in Fragile Cargo, then they are automatically the ritualist but their channeller ignores any unsaved wounds or mortal wounds on rolls of 4 or more instead of 5 or more.

TO THE VICTOR, THE SPOILS!

The winner earns an extra 3D6 renown.

5. EMPOWERED BY DEATH

Imbued with the power of the soul well, your leader catches glimpses of a spectre directing your warband towards a great and powerful relic. Your rival will stop at nothing to prevent you reaching this treasure.

Play Assassinate on page 26. If one of the players was victorious in Vortex of Power, then they are automatically the target and they can add D3 to their general's Wounds characteristic for the duration of the game.

TO THE VICTOR, THE SPOILS!

The winner can randomly generate a command ability from the Command Abilities table on page 17. If the winner achieved a **major victory**, then once per battle in their hero phase, their general can use this command ability in addition to any others they can use.

6. BONESTORM

A raging bonestorm is closing in. You must reach the relic before it is buried beneath the dunes forever, and stop your rival from taking it!

Play Seize the Relic on page 27. The player who was victorious in Assassinate chooses who has the first turn in the first battle round, regardless of who finishes setting up first.

TO THE VICTOR, THE SPOILS!

The winner of this game is the overall winner of the campaign!

SKIRMISH MATCHED PLAY

In the Mortal Realms, warbands come in all shapes and sizes, but to truly test a general's mettle as a commander, there needs to be a level playing field. This is the goal of matched play.

Matched play games are both challenging and rewarding. A battle between evenly balanced warbands makes for a decisive test of your strategic skills, and the outcome of such a clash will always be hard to predict.

The renown system on pages 35-40 has been designed to allow you and your opponent to assemble your warbands based on a prearranged points total, ensuring that your forces are as evenly matched as possible. Once you have settled on your warband's composition, you essentially have a pick-up-and-play force that you can bring to any table, against any opponent. For this reason, matched play is ideal for school leagues and tournaments, as putting a limit on the size of the warbands makes it easier to control how long a game will last. By the same token, matched play is perfect for a quick game in your local Warhammer store.

Matched play Skirmish games use the same rules as any other game of *Warhammer Age of Sigmar: Skirmish*, with the following modifications and suggestions.

MATCHED PLAY BATTLEPLANS

Below are the three battleplans that are best suited to an even Skirmish battle. Players can either choose which one to play or roll on the following table:

D6	Battleplan
1-2	Clash at Dawn (pg 22)
3-4	Treasure Hunt (pg 23)
5-6	Seize the Relic (pg 27)

You can also use any of the battleplans in the 'Matched Play Games' section of the *General's Handbook* simply by altering the size of the board to a 4'x4' area and adjusting the distance between objectives appropriately. All of these battleplans have been designed to present both players with matching objectives and territories, as well as a variety of tactical options.

PICK-UP GAMES

For pick-up games, we recommend following the suggestions in the 'Choosing a Warband' section of this book (pg 34). This gives guidelines for how long different sizes of game may take, allowing you and your opponent to tailor the game to suit the amount of time you have to play and the number of models you have available.

TOURNAMENTS

For tournament play, we recommend warbands with a starting value of 50 renown. You could allow players to follow the 'Between Games' sequence on page 18, and for each subsequent game you could increase the total renown value of fighters which each player may set up on the battlefield by a fixed amount. For example, the warband size for Game 2 might be 60 renown, for Game 3 it might be 70 renown and so on. This may mean that some players cannot use their whole warband in a particular battle, but will give these players a wider array of models to choose from. You should be able to play around five or six games over the course of a day, allowing you to play a variety of battleplans.

There are several different ways to determine the winner of a tournament. For example, ultimate victory might go to the player who has earned the most renown over a set number of games, or you may wish to assign the following victory point values to each game result:

Your Result	Victory Points
Major Victory	30
Minor Victory	20
Draw	10
Loss	5

HOUSE RULES

There are countless ways to customise your games. You may wish to place restrictions on certain types of unit, e.g. those with missile weapons with a range of greater than 12", or only allow players to include a single WIZARD in their warband. Each of these tweaks to the rules can provide a new and interesting challenge to players and add greater variety to your games of *Warhammer Age of Sigmar: Skirmish*.

SKIRMISH BATTLE:
CLASH AT DAWN

Travelling at nighttime is fraught with peril; warbands scouring the same territory may cross paths without even realising it. As dawn breaks, rival formations are revealed to be dangerously entangled, and the ensuing battle is brutal and chaotic.

THE WARBANDS
The players choose their warbands as described on page 34.

THE BATTLEFIELD
Set up the scenery for the battle as described on the *Warhammer Age of Sigmar* rules sheet.

SET-UP
Both players roll a dice, re-rolling in the case of a tie. The players alternate setting up models one at a time as described below, starting with the player that rolled highest. If one player finishes first, the opposing player must set up the rest of their models, one after the other. The player that finishes setting up first chooses who has the first turn in the first battle round.

THE FOG OF WAR
The battlefield is divided into table quarters, as shown on the map. Before each model is set up, you must roll a dice for it and consult the map to see which quarter of the battlefield it must be set up in. If a 5 or 6 is rolled, or it is not possible to set up a model in the quarter you have rolled, the player may choose which quarter that model is set up in. Models may not be set up in the area marked as No Man's Land, but may otherwise be deployed anywhere wholly in that quarter and more than 9" from enemy models. Any models that cannot be set up in this way are placed to one side and will arrive as reinforcements later in the game.

REINFORCEMENTS
You may bring on any reinforcements at the end of any of your movement phases; place these models within 3" of any edge of the battlefield and more than 9" from any enemy models. Reinforcements that have not arrived by the start of the third battle round count as slain for victory purposes.

THE BREAK OF DAWN
In the first battle round, line of sight is limited to 12". Models may only shoot, charge and use abilities and spells up to this distance. In the second battle round, this distance increases to 18". This effect ends at the end of the second battle round.

VICTORY
Do not use any of the victory conditions from the *Warhammer Age of Sigmar* rules sheet.

The game ends at the end of any battle round in which at least one player's warband has been broken. A warband is broken when more than half of its models have been slain or have fled.

If, at the end of the game, one player's warband is broken and their general has been slain, their opponent wins a **major victory**. If one player's warband is broken but their general is still on the battlefield, their opponent wins a **minor victory**. If both players' warbands are broken, the result is a **draw**.

SKIRMISH BATTLE:
TREASURE HUNT

When a report is received of a location where powerful artefacts may be hidden, a small, self-sufficient band of warriors is usually sent to investigate. When two opposing factions receive the same intelligence however, what started out as reconnaisance becomes a frantic scramble to secure treasures before the enemy can do the same.

THE WARBANDS

The players choose their warbands as described on page 34.

THE BATTLEFIELD

Set up the scenery for the battle as described on the *Warhammer Age of Sigmar* rules sheet.

HIDDEN WEALTH

The battlefield features five hoards, as shown on the map. Use appropriate terrain from your collection to represent them.

SET-UP

Both players roll a dice, re-rolling in the case of a tie, and the player that rolls higher decides whether to be the looter or the pillager. The territories for the two warbands are shown on the map.

The players alternate setting up models one at a time, starting with the player that won the dice roll to determine territories. Models must be set up in their own territory.

Continue to set up models until both players have set up their warbands. If one player finishes first, the opposing player must set up the rest of their models, one after the other. The player that finishes setting up first chooses who has the first turn in the first battle round.

SEARCHING FOR ARTEFACTS

At the end of each of your movement phases, you may roll a dice for each hoard that is within 3" of any of your models. On a roll of 6, an artefact has been uncovered at that hoard. Players may continue to search hoards in their own turn until an artefact is discovered at that hoard, at which point no further rolls are made for that hoard. A player controls an artefact if they have more models within 3" of that hoard than their opponent.

VICTORY

Do not use any of the victory conditions from the *Warhammer Age of Sigmar* rules sheet.

If one player wipes out their opponent's warband, the game ends immediately and they win a **major victory**. Otherwise, the game lasts for five battle rounds. If one player controls any artefacts at the end of the game (see left) and their opponent controls none, they win a **major victory**. If both players control artefacts, the player who controls the most wins a **minor victory**. If both players control the same number of artefacts, or neither player controls any artefacts, the result is a **draw**.

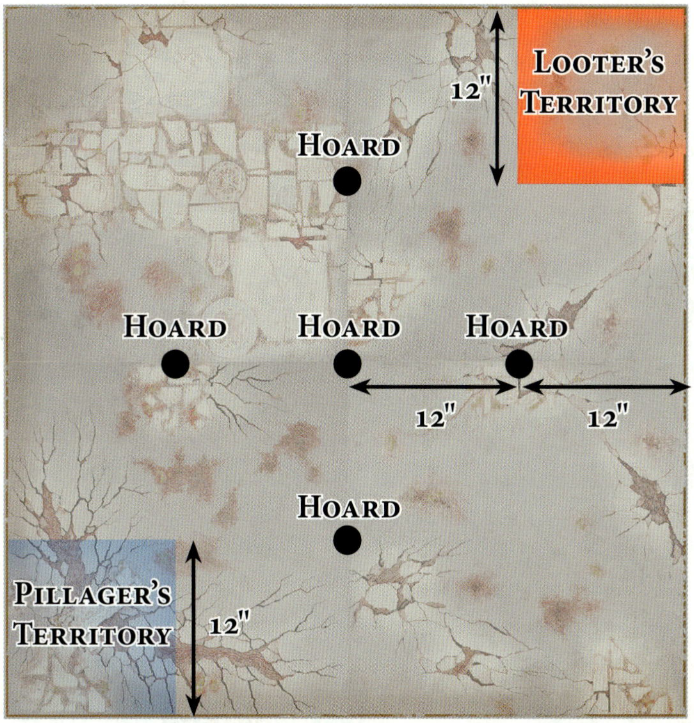

SKIRMISH BATTLE:
FRAGILE CARGO

A warband in possession of precious cargo is an irresistible target – not only is their attention focused on guarding their prize, thus rendering them vulnerable, but an ambusher may secure the haul for themselves in addition to slaying their quarry. However, it is unlikely that the cargo's guardian will give it up without a fight…

THE WARBANDS
The players choose their warbands as described on page 34.

THE BATTLEFIELD
Set up the scenery for the battle as described on the *Warhammer Age of Sigmar* rules sheet.

SET-UP
Both players roll a dice, re-rolling in the case of a tie, and the player that rolls higher decides whether to be the guard or the interceptor. The territories for the two warbands are shown on the map.

Designer's Note: *The faded area of the guard's territory is only used in a campaign.*

THE CARGO
The guard must pick one of their models to be the bearer of the cargo (use a suitable counter to represent the cargo itself), before placing the bearer in the centre of their territory. They must then set up the rest of their models anywhere within their territory. The interceptor then sets up all of their models anywhere within their territory. The guard chooses who has the first turn in the first battle round.

The bearer of the cargo may not run or charge, but may shoot, pile in and fight in the combat phase as normal. If the bearer is slain or removed from the battlefield for any reason, then the guard must place the cargo anywhere within 3" of the bearer before the model is removed. Should this happen, then at the end of any of their following movement phases, the guard can select another bearer from any of their models that have ended their move within 1" of the cargo.

VICTORY
Do not use any of the victory conditions from the *Warhammer Age of Sigmar* rules sheet.

If one player wipes out their opponent's warband, the game ends immediately and they win a **major victory**.

Otherwise the game lasts for six battle rounds. If, at the end of the game, the bearer of the cargo is wholly within the interceptor's territory (see map), the guard wins a **minor victory**.

However, if the bearer of the cargo escapes the battlefield by moving off the interceptor's edge of the battlefield (see map), the guard wins a **major victory** instead.

If the cargo is within the interceptor's territory at the end of the game but has no bearer, the result is a **draw**. If the cargo is outside of the interceptor's territory at the end of the game, the interceptor wins a **minor victory**, unless it also has no bearer, in which case the interceptor wins a **major victory**.

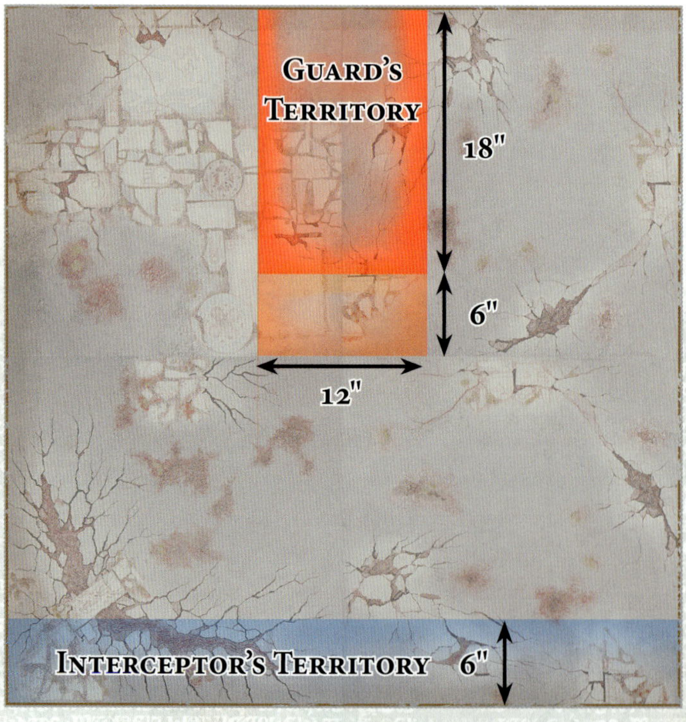

INTERCEPTOR'S TABLE EDGE

SKIRMISH BATTLE:
VORTEX OF POWER

In smaller engagements, the influence of spellcasters and god-touched souls is often magnified a hundredfold. The act of harnessing otherworldly forces usually involves a complex spell or a lengthy supplication however – a window of opportunity that the enemy will exploit to bring a halt to the ritual that would see them undone.

THE WARBANDS

The players choose their warbands as described on page 34.

THE BATTLEFIELD

Set up the scenery for the battle as described on the *Warhammer Age of Sigmar* rules sheet.

SWIRLING VORTEX

The centre of the battlefield (see map) represents a swirling vortex of power. Roll a dice each time a model moves through, into or remains within the vortex during their movement phase; on a roll of 1, 2 or 3 the model being rolled for suffers D3 mortal wounds from the roiling energies. In addition, players must subtract 2 from any hit rolls they make for ranged attacks in the shooting phase that pass through the vortex's boundary.

SET-UP

Both players roll a dice, re-rolling in the case of a tie, and the player that rolls higher decides whether to be the ritualist or the disrupter. The territories for the two warbands are shown on the map.

THE CHANNELLER

The ritualist must pick their general or a PRIEST or WIZARD from their warband to be the channeller of the vortex, before placing the channeller anywhere in their territory that is within 1" of the vortex. They must then set up the rest of their models anywhere within their territory. The disrupter then sets up all of their models anywhere within their territory.

The disrupter chooses who has the first turn in the first battle round.

The channeller cannot be moved further than 1" away from the vortex under any circumstances, but may otherwise act normally. However, the channeller can draw otherworldly strength from the vortex's magical energies – the ritualist can roll a dice each time the channeller suffers an unsaved wound or mortal wound; on a roll of 5 or more, that wound is ignored.

VICTORY

Do not use any of the victory conditions from the *Warhammer Age of Sigmar* rules sheet.

If one player wipes out their opponent's warband, the game ends immediately and they win a **major victory**. Otherwise the game lasts for five battle rounds. If, at the end of the game, the channeller is still on the battlefield, the ritualist wins a **major victory**, unless their general has suffered at least three unsaved wounds or mortal wounds, in which case they win a **minor victory** instead. If the channeller has been slain, the disrupter wins a **major victory**, unless their general has been slain, in which case they win a **minor victory** instead. If the channeller has been slain but the disrupter's warband has been wiped out, the result is a **draw**.

SKIRMISH BATTLE:
ASSASSINATE

An encamped warband is a stubborn target. A canny attacker knows that a prolonged conflict with such a foe should be avoided; it is better to act swiftly and pierce the beating heart of the warband – the leader around which they rally.

THE WARBANDS
The players choose their warbands as described on page 34.

THE BATTLEFIELD
Set up the scenery for the battle as described on the *Warhammer Age of Sigmar* rules sheet.

THE ENCAMPMENT
The battlefield features an encampment, as shown on the map – use appropriate terrain from your collection to represent this.

SET-UP
Both players roll a dice, re-rolling in the case of a tie, and the player that rolls higher decides whether to be the assassin or the target. The warbands' territories are shown on the map.

The players alternate setting up models one at a time, starting with the player that won the dice roll to determine territories. Models must be set up in their own territory.

Continue to set up models until both players have set up their warbands. If one player finishes first, the opposing player must set up the rest of their models, one after the other. The player that finishes setting up first chooses who has the first turn in the first battle round.

A REPUTATION TO MAINTAIN
This is the target's encampment and their general will not abandon it without a fight. The target's general cannot move beyond the encampment's boundaries under any circumstances, but may otherwise act normally.

VICTORY
Do not use any of the victory conditions from the *Warhammer Age of Sigmar* rules sheet.

The target's general is the assassin's mark. If the assassin slays the mark, the game ends immediately and they win a **major victory**, unless the assassin's general has also been slain, in which case they win a **minor victory** instead. If the target wipes out the assassin's warband, the game ends immediately and they win a **major victory**.

Otherwise, the game lasts for five battle rounds. If, at the end of the game, the mark is still on the battlefield, the target wins a **major victory**, unless their general has suffered at least three unsaved wounds or mortal wounds, in which case they win a **minor victory** instead.

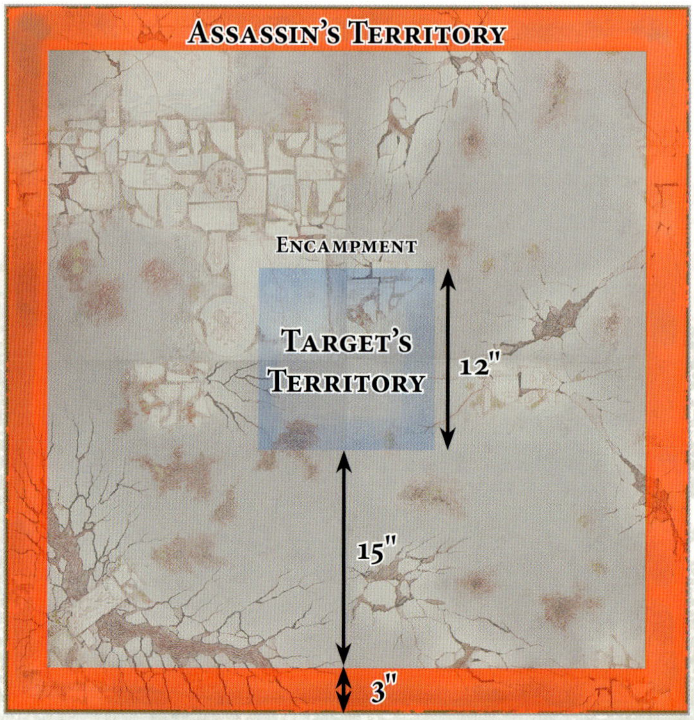

SKIRMISH BATTLE:
SEIZE THE RELIC

Those relics of great power that lie unclaimed within the realms are often just so because they reside in locations of great peril – perhaps the eye of a magical storm or a derelict temple surrounded by roaming predators. To linger in the vicinity of the prize is to court death – seize it and escape before the enemy or the realms themselves claim your warriors' lives!

THE WARBANDS

The players choose their warbands as described on page 34.

THE BATTLEFIELD

Set up the scenery for the battle as described on the *Warhammer Age of Sigmar* rules sheet.

THE SANCTUARY

The battlefield features a sanctuary with two entrances 2-3" wide as shown on the map. The sanctuary can only be accessed through these entrances; the boundaries of the sanctuary are impassable and block line of sight. At the centre of the sanctuary is an altar upon which rests a relic of unimaginable power.

SET-UP

Both players roll a dice, re-rolling in the case of a tie, and the player that rolls higher decides whether to be the plunderer or the relic hunter. The territories for the two warbands are shown on the map.

The players alternate setting up models one at a time, starting with the player that won the dice roll to determine territories. Models must be set up in their own territory.

Continue to set up models until both players have set up their warbands. If one player finishes first, the opposing player must set up the rest of their models, one after the other. The player that finishes setting up first chooses who has the first turn in the first battle round.

ARCANE STORM

Any models that have not reached the safety of the sanctuary will face the fury of the arcane storm. At the end of the first battle round, any models within 6" of the plunderer's or relic hunter's edge of the battlefield (see map) immediately suffer D3 mortal wounds. At the end of the second battle round, the distance of this effect is increased to 12", and at the end of the third battle round, it is increased to 18". At the end of the fourth and subsequent battle rounds, any models that are not wholly within the sanctuary suffer D3 mortal wounds.

VICTORY

Do not use any of the victory conditions from the *Warhammer Age of Sigmar* rules sheet.

If one player wipes out their opponent's warband, the game ends immediately and they win a **major victory**. If, at the end of the fifth battle round, one player has a greater number of models within 3" of the altar, the game ends immediately and they win a **major victory**. If there are an equal number of models belonging to each player within 3" of the altar at the end of the fifth battle round, continue playing until one player has a greater number of models within 3" of the altar at the end of any subsequent battle round; once this condition is met, the game ends immediately and that player wins a **minor victory**.

Eager to slay worthy opponents, a skull-hunting party of Khorne Bloodbound falls upon a group of Stormcast Eternals.

The Knight-Questor stands defiant as his brethren mete out their righteous fury on the worshippers of the Blood God.

Desolate ruins become splattered with gore as the corpse-eaters pounce upon their Khornate foe.

This Flesh-eater Court sees Shadespire as an unspoilt paradise populated with savage tribes who guard its myriad riches.

Prosecutors join the Stormcast Eternals as they cross blades with two other warbands in the city's endless crypts.

Lingering death magic mingles with Waaagh! energy as orruks and mordants meet in the crumbling streets.

War cries echo through the haunted city as treasure hunters, glory seekers and brutal butchers charge into combat.

Death comes from all directions – chasms gape underfoot and choking clouds billow forth on the Wailing Wind.

To these Ironjawz, Shadespire is but an endless battleground, and its treasures a lure to draw in fresh warbands.

CHOOSING A WARBAND

Warbands can vary wildly in size and composition, ranging from a motley trio of heroes to a marauding horde of warriors following their chieftain's lead. The rules here describe how to select your very own warband in preparation for its first quest.

The first step in choosing your warband is to decide which of the four Grand Alliances your warband will hail from: Order, Chaos, Death or Destruction.

Next, you must choose the models that will make up your warband. The size of your warband will depend on its renown. If you are planning to play a one-off game, we recommend that each player chooses a warband of equal renown, ranging anywhere between 50-100 renown. Obviously the size of the warband you choose will have an effect on the average length of the game; you should be able to play a Skirmish Battle featuring 50-renown warbands in less than an hour, whilst a similar game with 100-renown warbands will likely take 90 minutes or maybe even longer.

If you are playing a campaign (see pages 18-20), we suggest that each player chooses a starting warband with a renown of 25, as it will grow in size as the campaign unfolds.

Regardless of its total renown, you must adhere to the following restrictions when choosing your warband:

- All models in a warband must be drawn from the same Grand Alliance.
- Your warband must include a minimum of three models, one of which must be a HERO to be the general of your warband.
- You may ignore the minimum unit size requirements on a warscroll – all count as having a minimum unit size of 1 model. For example, you may purchase 5 Gors at the cost listed in this section, rather than the usual minimum of 10 on their warscroll.
- You may choose any combination of weapon options for models from the same warscroll. For example, you may take an Orruk Brute armed with two Brute Choppas, as well as an Orruk Brute armed with a Jagged Gore-hacka. However, you must adhere to any limitations on weapon options that are otherwise specified. For example, only 1 in 5 Orruk Brutes can be armed with a Massive Gore-choppa, regardless of the weapon combination of the other models from the same warscroll.
- You may only include each warscroll once in your warband.
- You may only take each champion model (such as a Liberator-Prime) once per warscroll.
- Your warband may not incorporate any warscroll battalions, even if your warband would otherwise fulfil the battalion's organisation requirements.

CHAOS

BRAYHERDS

UNIT	UNIT SIZE MIN	UNIT SIZE MAX	RENOWN PER MODEL
Gors	1	10	2
Ungors	1	20	1
Great Bray-Shaman	1	1	18
Bestigors	1	10	3
Ungor Raiders	1	20	2

CLANS ESHIN

UNIT	UNIT SIZE MIN	UNIT SIZE MAX	RENOWN PER MODEL
Deathrunner	1	1	24
Night Runners	1	20	2

CLANS MOULDER

UNIT	UNIT SIZE MIN	UNIT SIZE MAX	RENOWN PER MODEL
Packmaster	1	1	16
Giant Rats	1	20	1
Rat Ogors	1	3	12

CLANS PESTILENS

UNIT	UNIT SIZE MIN	UNIT SIZE MAX	RENOWN PER MODEL
Plague Priest with Warpstone-tipped Staff	1	1	16
Plague Monks	1	20	1

CLANS SKRYRE

UNIT	UNIT SIZE MIN	UNIT SIZE MAX	RENOWN PER MODEL
Doomwheel	1	1	26
Warlock Engineer	1	1	20
Warpfire Thrower Weapon Team	1	1	14
Poisoned Wind Mortar Weapon Team	1	1	12
Stormfiend	1	1	20

CLANS VERMINUS

UNIT	UNIT SIZE MIN	UNIT SIZE MAX	RENOWN PER MODEL
Clanrats	1	20	1
Skaven Warlord	1	1	20
Stormvermin	1	10	3

DAEMONS OF KHORNE

UNIT	UNIT SIZE MIN	UNIT SIZE MAX	RENOWN PER MODEL
Bloodletters	1	10	2
Bloodmaster, Herald of Khorne	1	1	16
Blood Throne	1	1	24
Bloodcrushers	1	3	11

DAEMONS OF NURGLE

UNIT	UNIT SIZE MIN	UNIT SIZE MAX	RENOWN PER MODEL
Plaguebearers	1	10	2
Herald of Nurgle	1	1	20
Nurglings	1	3	5
Plague Drone	1	1	15

DAEMONS OF TZEENTCH

UNIT	UNIT SIZE MIN	UNIT SIZE MAX	RENOWN PER MODEL
Pink Horrors	1	10	3
Herald of Tzeentch	1	1	24
The Changeling	1	1	28
Exalted Flamer	1	1	24
Flamers	1	3	12
Screamers	1	3	8
Blue Horrors	1	20	1
Brimstone Horrors	1	20	1

EVERCHOSEN

UNIT	UNIT SIZE MIN	UNIT SIZE MAX	RENOWN PER MODEL
Gaunt Summoner of Tzeentch	1	1	24
Varanguard	1	1	20

HOSTS OF SLAANESH

UNIT	UNIT SIZE MIN	UNIT SIZE MAX	RENOWN PER MODEL
Daemonettes	1	10	2
Herald of Slaanesh	1	1	12
Herald of Slaanesh on Seeker Chariot	1	1	20
Exalted Seeker Chariot	1	1	28
Hellflayer of Slaanesh	1	1	16
Hellstriders of Slaanesh	1	5	4
Seeker Chariot	1	1	16
Seekers of Slaanesh	1	5	5

KHORNE BLOODBOUND

UNIT	UNIT SIZE MIN	UNIT SIZE MAX	RENOWN PER MODEL
Blood Warriors	1	10	4
Bloodreavers	1	20	1
Aspiring Deathbringer	1	1	16
Aspiring Deathbringer with Goreaxe & Skullhammer	1	1	20
Bloodsecrator	1	1	24
Bloodstoker	1	1	16
Exalted Deathbringer	1	1	16
Exalted Deathbringer with Impaling Spear	1	1	16
Mighty Lord of Khorne	1	1	28
Skullgrinder	1	1	16
Slaughterpriest	1	1	20
Slaughterpriest with Hackblade & Wrath-hammer	1	1	20
Mighty Skullcrushers	1	3	9
Skullreapers	1	5	7
Wrathmongers	1	5	7
Khorgorath	1	1	16

MASTERCLAN

UNIT	UNIT SIZE MIN	UNIT SIZE MAX	RENOWN PER MODEL
Grey Seer	1	1	24

NURGLE ROTBRINGERS

UNIT	UNIT SIZE MIN	UNIT SIZE MAX	RENOWN PER MODEL
Gutrot Spume	1	1	24
Lord of Plagues	1	1	20
Putrid Blightkings	1	5	7

THUNDERSCORN

UNIT	UNIT SIZE MIN	UNIT SIZE MAX	RENOWN PER MODEL
Dragon Ogors	1	3	11

SLAVES TO DARKNESS

UNIT	UNIT SIZE MIN	UNIT SIZE MAX	RENOWN PER MODEL
Chaos Marauders	1	20	1
Chaos Warriors	1	10	4
Darkoath Chieftain	1	1	16
Lord of Chaos	1	1	20
Chaos Chariot	1	1	16
Chaos Gorebeast Chariot	1	1	20
Chaos Knights	1	5	6
Chaos Marauder Horsemen	1	10	4
Chaos Spawn	1	1	10

TZEENTCH ARCANITES

UNIT	UNIT SIZE MIN	UNIT SIZE MAX	RENOWN PER MODEL
Kairic Acolytes	10	40	3
Tzaangors	10	30	4
Gaunt Summoner & Chaos Familiars	1	1	24
Gaunt Summoner	1	1	20
Magister	1	1	24
Tzaangor Shaman	1	1	24
Tzaangor Enlightened	1	3	11
Tzaangor Skyfires	1	3	11

WARHERDS

UNIT	UNIT SIZE MIN	UNIT SIZE MAX	RENOWN PER MODEL
Bullgors	1	3	12

MONSTERS OF CHAOS

UNIT	UNIT SIZE MIN	UNIT SIZE MAX	RENOWN PER MODEL
Chaos Warhounds	1	10	2

DEATH

DEADWALKERS

UNIT	UNIT SIZE MIN	UNIT SIZE MAX	RENOWN PER MODEL
Dire Wolves	1	10	2
Zombies	1	30	1
Corpse Cart	1	1	16

DEATHMAGES

UNIT	UNIT SIZE MIN	UNIT SIZE MAX	RENOWN PER MODEL
Necromancer	1	1	22

DEATHRATTLE

UNIT	UNIT SIZE MIN	UNIT SIZE MAX	RENOWN PER MODEL
Skeleton Warriors	1	20	2
Wight King with Baleful Tomb Blade	1	1	24
Black Knights	1	5	5
Grave Guard	1	10	3

FLESH-EATER COURTS

UNIT	UNIT SIZE MIN	UNIT SIZE MAX	RENOWN PER MODEL
Crypt Ghouls	1	20	2
Abhorrant Ghoul King	1	1	24
Crypt Ghast Courtier	1	1	16
Crypt Haunter Courtier	1	1	24
Crypt Infernal Courtier	1	1	28
Crypt Flayers	1	3	11
Crypt Horrors	1	3	11

NIGHTHAUNT

UNIT	UNIT SIZE MIN	UNIT SIZE MAX	RENOWN PER MODEL
Cairn Wraith	1	1	12
Tomb Banshee	1	1	16
Hexwraiths	1	5	6
Spirit Hosts	1	3	8

SOULBLIGHT

UNIT	UNIT SIZE MIN	UNIT SIZE MAX	RENOWN PER MODEL
Vargheists	1	3	11

DESTRUCTION

BEASTCLAW RAIDERS

UNIT	UNIT SIZE MIN	UNIT SIZE MAX	RENOWN PER MODEL
Mournfang Pack	1	2	16

BONESPLITTERZ

UNIT	UNIT SIZE MIN	UNIT SIZE MAX	RENOWN PER MODEL
Savage Orruks	1	20	2
Savage Big Boss	1	1	24
Savage Big Stabbas	1	2	10
Savage Boarboy Maniaks	1	10	6
Savage Boarboys	1	10	5
Savage Orruk Arrowboys	1	20	2
Savage Orruk Morboys	1	20	2

GUTBUSTERS

UNIT	UNIT SIZE MIN	UNIT SIZE MAX	RENOWN PER MODEL
Grot Scraplauncher	1	1	26
Ironblaster	1	1	28
Ogors	1	6	8
Grots	1	30	1
Ironguts	1	3	13
Leadbelchers	1	3	9

MOONCLAN GROTS

UNIT	UNIT SIZE MIN	UNIT SIZE MAX	RENOWN PER MODEL
Grots	1	30	1

GITMOB GROTS

Unit	Unit Size Min	Unit Size Max	Renown per Model
Grots	1	30	1
Grot Shaman	1	1	16
Grot Wolf Riders	1	10	4

GREENSKINZ

Unit	Unit Size Min	Unit Size Max	Renown per Model
Orruks	1	20	2
Orruk Boarboys	1	10	4
Orruk Boar Chariot	1	1	16

SPIDERFANG GROTS

Unit	Unit Size Min	Unit Size Max	Renown per Model
Grot Spider Riders	1	10	4

IRONJAWZ

Unit	Unit Size Min	Unit Size Max	Renown per Model
Orruk Megaboss	1	1	28
Orruk Warchanter	1	1	16
Orruk Weirdnob Shaman	1	1	24
Orruk Ardboys	1	10	4
Orruk Brutes	1	5	7
Orruk Gore-gruntas	1	3	9

TROGGOTHS

Unit	Unit Size Min	Unit Size Max	Renown per Model
Fellwater Troggoths	1	3	12

ORDER

DARKLING COVENS

Unit	Unit Size Min	Unit Size Max	Renown per Model
Bleakswords	1	20	2
Darkshards	1	20	2
Dreadspears	1	20	2
Sorceress	1	1	16
Black Guard	1	10	3
Executioners	1	10	3

DAUGHTERS OF KHAINE

Unit	Unit Size Min	Unit Size Max	Renown per Model
Death Hag	1	1	12
Bloodwrack Medusa	1	1	24
Doomfire Warlocks	1	5	6
Sisters of Slaughter	1	10	3
Witch Aelves	1	20	2

COLLEGIATE ARCANE

Unit	Unit Size Min	Unit Size Max	Renown per Model
Battlemage	1	1	20

ELDRITCH COUNCIL

Unit	Unit Size Min	Unit Size Max	Renown per Model
Archmage	1	1	24
Loremaster	1	1	20
Swordmasters	1	10	3

FREE PEOPLES

Unit	Unit Size Min	Unit Size Max	Renown per Model
Freeguild Archers	1	20	2
Freeguild Crossbowmen	1	20	2
Freeguild Guard	1	20	2
Freeguild Handgunners	1	20	2
Freeguild General	1	1	20
Demigryph Knights	1	3	11
Freeguild Greatswords	1	10	3
Freeguild Outriders	1	5	5
Freeguild Pistoliers	1	5	5

LION RANGERS

Unit	Unit Size Min	Unit Size Max	Renown per Model
White Lion Chariot	1	1	20
White Lions	1	10	3

DISPOSSESSED

UNIT	UNIT SIZE MIN	UNIT SIZE MAX	RENOWN PER MODEL
Warriors	1	20	2
Longbeards	1	20	2
Runelord	1	1	16
Unforged	1	1	20
Warden King	1	1	24
Hammerers	1	10	4
Ironbreakers	1	10	3
Irondrakes	1	10	4
Quarrellers	1	20	2
Thunderers	1	20	2

FYRESLAYERS

UNIT	UNIT SIZE MIN	UNIT SIZE MAX	RENOWN PER MODEL
Vulkite Berzerkers	1	20	2
Auric Runefather	1	1	16
Auric Runemaster	1	1	16
Auric Runesmiter	1	1	16
Auric Runeson	1	1	16
Battlesmith	1	1	16
Doomseeker	1	1	16
Grimwrath Berzerker	1	1	16
Auric Hearthguard	1	10	3
Hearthguard Berzerkers	1	10	3

IRONWELD ARSENAL

UNIT	UNIT SIZE MIN	UNIT SIZE MAX	RENOWN PER MODEL
Cogsmith	1	1	20
Gunmaster	1	1	16
Gyrobomber	1	1	16
Gyrocopter	1	1	16

KHARADRON OVERLORDS

UNIT	UNIT SIZE MIN	UNIT SIZE MAX	RENOWN PER MODEL
Arkanaut Company	1	20	2
Aether-Khemist	1	1	20
Aetheric Navigator	1	1	20
Arkanaut Admiral	1	1	28
Endrinmaster	1	1	16
Endrinriggers	1	3	8
Grundstok Thunderers	1	10	4
Skywardens	1	3	7

SCOURGE PRIVATEERS

UNIT	UNIT SIZE MIN	UNIT SIZE MAX	RENOWN PER MODEL
Black Ark Fleetmaster	1	1	8
Black Ark Corsairs	1	20	2
Scourgerunner Chariot	1	1	20

SERAPHON

UNIT	UNIT SIZE MIN	UNIT SIZE MAX	RENOWN PER MODEL
Saurus Warriors	1	20	2
Skinks	1	20	1
Saurus Oldblood	1	1	24
Skink Starpriest	1	1	16
Ripperdactyl Riders	1	3	9
Saurus Guard	1	10	4
Saurus Knights	1	5	4
Terradon Riders	1	3	8

ORDER DRACONIS

UNIT	UNIT SIZE MIN	UNIT SIZE MAX	RENOWN PER MODEL
Dragon Noble	1	1	20
Dragon Blades	1	5	6

ORDER SERPENTIS

UNIT	UNIT SIZE MIN	UNIT SIZE MAX	RENOWN PER MODEL
Drakespawn Chariot	1	1	20
Drakespawn Knights	1	5	6

PHOENIX TEMPLE

UNIT	UNIT SIZE MIN	UNIT SIZE MAX	RENOWN PER MODEL
Anointed	1	1	16
Phoenix Guard	1	10	3

SHADOWBLADES

UNIT	UNIT SIZE MIN	UNIT SIZE MAX	RENOWN PER MODEL
Assassin	1	1	16
Dark Riders	1	5	5

SWIFTHAWK AGENTS

UNIT	UNIT SIZE MIN	UNIT SIZE MAX	RENOWN PER MODEL
Reavers	1	5	6
Chariot	1	1	16
Shadow Warriors	1	10	4
Skycutter	1	1	24
Spireguard	1	20	2

SYLVANETH

UNIT	UNIT SIZE MIN	UNIT SIZE MAX	RENOWN PER MODEL
Dryads	1	20	2
Branchwych	1	1	16
Kurnoth Hunters	1	3	15
Spite-Revenants	1	10	3
Tree-Revenants	1	10	3

WANDERERS

UNIT	UNIT SIZE MIN	UNIT SIZE MAX	RENOWN PER MODEL
Glade Guard	1	20	2
Nomad Prince	1	1	16
Eternal Guard	1	20	2
Sisters of the Thorn	1	5	9
Sisters of the Watch	1	10	4
Wild Riders	1	5	6
Wildwood Rangers	1	10	4

STORMCAST ETERNALS

UNIT	UNIT SIZE MIN	UNIT SIZE MAX	RENOWN PER MODEL
Liberators	1	10	4
Knight-Azyros	1	1	16
Knight-Heraldor	1	1	24
Knight-Questor	1	1	20
Knight-Venator	1	1	24
Knight-Vexillor	1	1	28
Lord-Castellant	1	1	20
Lord-Celestant	1	1	20
Lord-Relictor	1	1	16
Lord-Veritant	1	1	24
Aetherwings	1	3	4
Concussors	1	2	28
Decimators	1	5	8
Desolators	1	2	24
Fulminators	1	2	24
Gryph-hounds	1	3	8
Judicators	1	10	6
Prosecutors with Celestial Hammers	1	6	7
Prosecutors with Stormcall Javelins	1	6	7
Protectors	1	5	8
Retributors	1	5	8
Tempestors	1	2	22
Vanguard-Hunters	1	10	6
Vanguard-Palladors	1	3	15
Vanguard-Raptors with Hurricane Crossbows	1	3	11
Vanguard-Raptors with Longstrike Crossbows	1	3	12